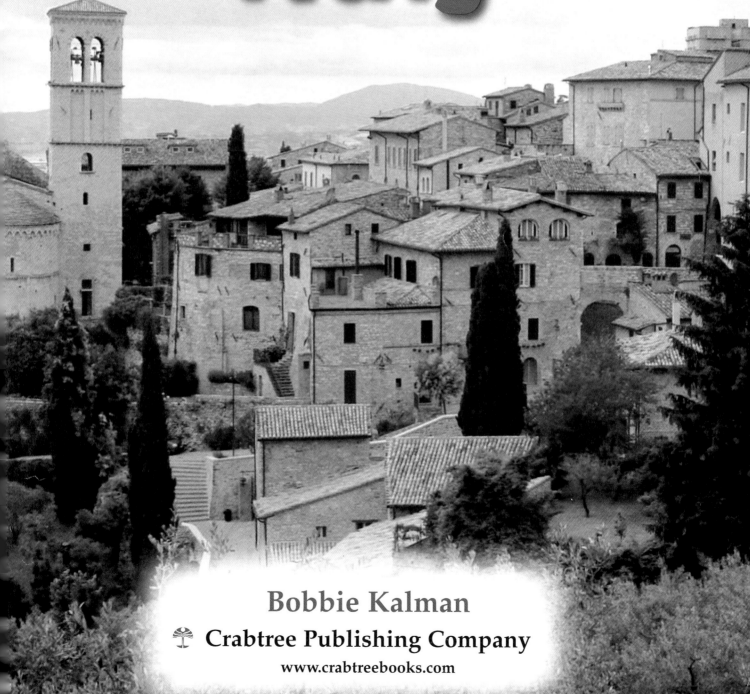

# Spotlight on
# Italy

Bobbie Kalman

Crabtree Publishing Company

www.crabtreebooks.com

# Spotlight On My Country

## Created by Bobbie Kalman

Dedicated by Katherine Berti
To the Berti family, with all my love.
Chi trova un amico, trova un tesoro.

**Author and Editor-in-Chief**
Bobbie Kalman

**Editors**
Kathy Middleton
Crystal Sikkens

**Fact editor**
Marcella Haanstra

**Design**
Bobbie Kalman
Katherine Berti
Samantha Crabtree (cover)

**Photo research**
Bobbie Kalman

**Print and production coordinator
and prepress technician**
Katherine Berti

**Photographs**
Dreamstime: pages 20 (top and bottom left),
    21 (except top right), 22 (top), 23 (bottom)
iStockphoto: page 21 (top right)
Photos.com: pages 11 (top), 13 (middle),
    27 (top), 29 (middle right)
Wikipedia: page 27 (bottom right);
    Gienouille vert: page 13 (bottom right)
Other images by Shutterstock

**Library and Archives Canada Cataloguing in Publication**

Kalman, Bobbie, 1947-
    Spotlight on Italy / Bobbie Kalman.

(Spotlight on my country)
Includes index.
Issued also in electronic format.
ISBN 978-0-7787-3462-8 (bound).--ISBN 978-0-7787-3488-8 (pbk.)

    1. Italy--Juvenile literature. I. Title. II. Series: Spotlight on
my country

DG417.K34 2011            j945            C2011-900001-6

**Library of Congress Cataloging-in-Publication Data**

Kalman, Bobbie.
  Spotlight on Italy / Bobbie Kalman.
    p. cm. -- (Spotlight on my country)
  Includes index.
  ISBN 978-0-7787-3488-8 (pbk. : alk. paper) -- ISBN 978-0-7787-3462-8
(reinforced library binding : alk. paper) -- ISBN 978-1-4271-9685-9
(electronic (pdf))
  1. Italy--Juvenile literature. I. Title. II. Series.

  DG417.K35 2011
  945--dc22
                                         2010051453

## Crabtree Publishing Company

www.crabtreebooks.com        1-800-387-7650

Printed in the U.S.A./022011/CJ20101228

**Published in Canada**
**Crabtree Publishing**
616 Welland Ave.
St. Catharines, Ontario
L2M 5V6

**Published in the United States**
**Crabtree Publishing**
PMB 59051
350 Fifth Avenue, 59th Floor
New York, New York 10118

**Published in the United Kingdom**
**Crabtree Publishing**
Maritime House
Basin Road North, Hove
BN41 1WR

**Published in Australia**
**Crabtree Publishing**
386 Mt. Alexander Rd.
Ascot Vale (Melbourne)
VIC 3032

# Contents

# Welcome to Italy!

Italy is part of the **continent** of Europe. A continent is a huge area of land. The other continents on Earth are Asia, Africa, North America, South America, Antarctica, and Australia/Oceania. The seven continents are shown on the map below. What are the names of Earth's five oceans?

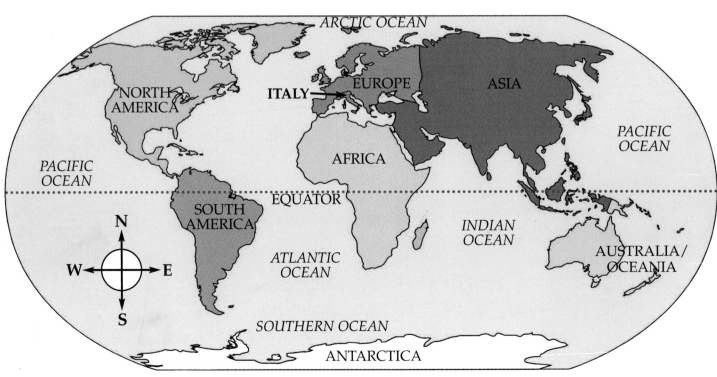

## Where is Italy?

Italy is a **country** in Europe. A country is an area of land with borders. Italy shares land borders with France, Switzerland, Austria, and Slovenia. Italy is a **peninsula**. A peninsula is a long, narrow strip of land that is surrounded by water on three sides. Italy juts out into the Mediterranean Sea. It looks like a boot that is kicking a stone. The "stone" is the **island** of Sicily. An island is land that has water all around it. Italy's capital city is Rome.

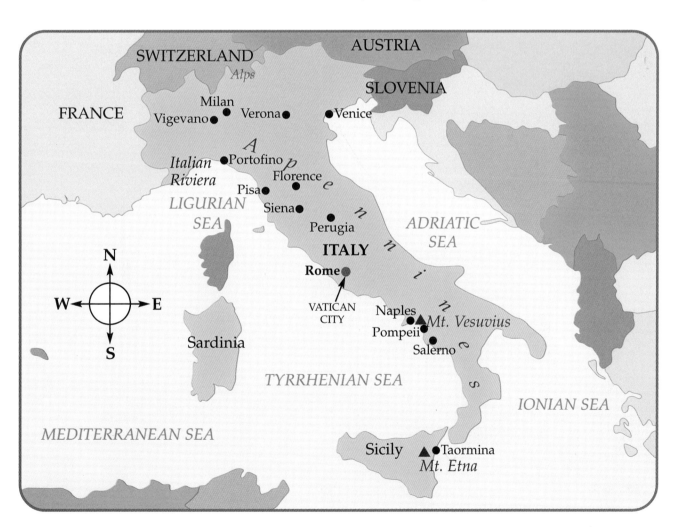

*The waters that surround most of Italy are the Adriatic Sea, Tyrrhenian Sea, Ligurian Sea, and Ionian Sea. They are all part of the Mediterranean Sea. A sea is an area of ocean close to land. The Mediterranean Sea is part of the Atlantic Ocean.*

5

# Islands of Italy

Italy's **coastline**, or line of **coasts**, stretches almost all the way around the country. Coasts are areas where land meets water. Most of Italy's coasts are rocky, but there are also many sandy beaches. Italy has islands, too. The largest are Sicily and Sardinia. Sicily sits about ten miles (16 km) from the southern tip of the peninsula. It is covered in mountains. Sardinia is smaller and farther from the mainland than Sicily is. Some of the island is mountainous, but more than half is made up of **pastures**, or lands covered in grass on which animals **graze**, or feed.

*Sardinia has beaches with white sand and clear blue ocean waters. Many people visit there each summer. Some sail their own boats, and some take cruise ships like these.*

cruise ships

Mount Etna

There are many **volcanic eruptions** on the island of Sicily. Europe's tallest **active volcano**, Mount Etna is on this island. Read about volcanoes on pages 10–11.

Greek theater

Taormina is a **historic** city in Sicily. It is located on the side of Mount Tauro. Many old buildings can be found throughout the town, such as the **ruins**, or remains, of a very old Greek theater.

# Italy's land

About three-quarters of Italy's land is made up of mountains and hills. Up in the north of the country, the Alps tower above the land. The tall mountains form natural borders between Italy and the countries next to it. Thick forests grow on the hills, and farmers grow crops or raise sheep in the **valleys**. Valleys are low areas between mountains.

*This happy girl is skiing on some very high mountains in the Italian Alps.*

*The Dolomites are part of the Alps. A village, or small town, sits at the bottom of these rocky mountains.*

*The Apennines mountain chain divides most of Italy. These mountains are not as high as the Alps. A castle sits on top of one of the mountains.*

*Most people live in the **lowlands**, or flat areas, of Italy. Cities and farms are in the lowlands.*

*Portofino is a village located in an area of the coast called the Italian Riviera. This popular area is visited by many tourists. Boats find shelter in its **harbor**, where the water is calm.*

# Volcanoes in Italy

Two of Italy's largest volcanoes are Mount Vesuvius and Mount Etna. Vesuvius is in the southern mainland of Italy, and Etna is in Sicily. Vesuvius **erupted** almost 2,000 years ago, destroying the cities of Pompeii and Herculaneum. Thousands of people died when they were buried under ash and mud. This picture shows Vesuvius, as well as the ruins of Pompeii.

*Mount Vesuvius*

*ruins of Pompeii*

*gases and ash*

*Lava is magma that has poured out of a volcano.*

*Earth's crust*

*magma*

A volcano is an opening in Earth's **crust**, or surface. When a volcano erupts, magma, rock, and ash burst out. An active volcano is one that has erupted recently or one that might erupt at any time. Vesuvius is thought to be a very dangerous active volcano because millions of people live near it. They live in the city of Naples and in the areas around the city.

## Dangerous Vesuvius!

Vesuvius has erupted many times. In 1631, more than 3,000 people died, and several villages were buried under lava. In 1906, the volcano shot out a huge amount of lava, killing many people. There have been no eruptions since 1944, but people who study volcanoes think that Vesuvius might erupt again.

*(right) When Vesuvius erupted in 1906, people grabbed whatever they could carry and ran for their lives.*

*Mount Etna is one of the most active volcanoes in the world. Like Vesuvius, it is dangerous because many people live near it on the island of Sicily. This picture shows Etna covered with snow.*

11

# Then and now

People have lived on the land that is now Italy for thousands of years. The Etruscans were among the first peoples in the north. People from Greece **settled**, or came to live, in the south at about the same time. Of all the cities, Rome grew to be the strongest. It became the center of a huge **empire**. An empire is a large group of countries ruled by one ruler. The Roman army took control of many lands in faraway places. After a few hundred years, the Roman Empire fell apart, and Italy belonged to different **kingdoms**. A kingdom is an area ruled by a king or queen.

*Is this Roman soldier looking for new lands for the Roman Empire to **conquer**, or take over?*

# The Republic of Italy

In 1860, Vittorio Emanuele II was successful in uniting all the kingdoms in Italy into one country. He became the king of the new Italy. There were many problems, and people did not agree on how to solve them. Two World Wars followed, making things worse in the country. With help from other countries, Italy recovered and voted to become a **republic** on June 2, 1946. Italians celebrate June 2 as Republic Day. In a republic, people vote for a president, who is the head of the country.

*The national flag of Italy has three colors—green, white, and red.*

*Military commander Giuseppe Garibaldi helped unite Italy. He is a national hero.*

*The Galleria Vittorio Emanuele II was built in honor of the king who united Italy into one country.*

*The President lives in Quirinale Palace.*

# The city of Rome

Rome is the capital city of Italy. It is also the center of art, business, and religion. Beautiful buildings and works of art are everywhere throughout the city. Rome is filled with statues, fountains, and *piazzas*, or town squares, where people gather to meet friends. At the Trevi Fountain, shown below, people throw coins into the water to ensure that they will return to Rome.

St. Peter's Basilica (church)

## Vatican City

Vatican City is a small country inside Rome. It is separate from Italy. The Vatican is the center of the Roman Catholic Church, which is a Christian religion. The **pope**, who is the head of the Church, and other Church leaders live in Vatican City. Each year, millions of Catholics come to receive the pope's blessing. St. Peter's Basilica is at the center of Vatican City. This huge church can hold 60,000 people!

*Many works of art are on the walls and ceilings of St. Peter's Basilica. It is a beautiful church!*

# Beautiful old cities

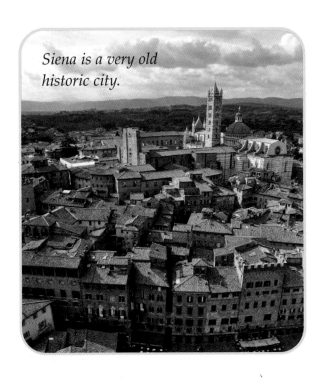

*Siena is a very old historic city.*

Many of Italy's cities are very old and beautiful. The city of Florence is known for its amazing works of art. Siena is famous for its *Palio*, a historic festival that takes place there (see page 23). Verona is a city filled with historic buildings, churches, and towers. Venice is the city of islands and **canals**, or waterways.

*Florence is in Tuscany, a beautiful region of Italy. Florence is known as the birthplace or home of famous artists such as Leonardo da Vinci, Botticelli, and Michelangelo. Learn more about these artists on pages 26–27.*

Verona is in northern Italy. Many people visit the city because of its fairs, shows, and music. Verona is also famous as the setting for the story of Romeo and Juliet. You can visit Juliet's balcony in Verona and hear her story.

Romeo and Juliet

Juliet's balcony

Venice is located on 118 small islands along the Adriatic Sea in northeast Italy. Instead of streets, Venice has canals. Each year, the people of Venice wear wonderful masks and costumes during Carnevale celebrations (see pages 24–25).

# The people of Italy

Most Italians speak the same language and share the same traditions, holidays, and religious beliefs. Italians are proud of their art, history, and food. They especially value their families. **Extended family** members, such as aunts, uncles, cousins, and grandparents, often get together for family dinners and special occasions. Some work together in family businesses. Italian families have strong ties and look after one another.

*These parents and their children are having a fun day in town. They enjoy being together.*

*Grandmother has made a big pan of pasta for lunch. Her grandchildren have come to visit.*

This family owns an olive-oil company. Olive oil is made from olives, which grow on olive trees. Almost all of the world's olive trees grow in the Mediterranean region. The mother and daughter on the left have picked a basket of olives. The olives will be put into presses, which squeeze the oil from them.

In Italy, you are never far from a sea. This family enjoys going for boat rides.

# Italy's children

Italian children go to elementary school and high school. Many also go on to university. Until recently, most children went to school six days a week. Many schools have now switched to a five-day week. After school, children play sports, do homework, or spend time with family or friends. They also take part in religious and historic festivals. Many live near water and go swimming in the summer.

*Italian children enjoy playing ball games such as rugby and soccer. The boy on the left and the ones top left are playing rugby. The boys above are on their way to a soccer game. Their shirts are the same colors as two of the three colors in Italy's flag. What is the flag's third color?*

Religious ceremonies, such as **first communion**, are special times for children. The children wear white gowns. After the church service, families have big parties with food, gifts, and fun.

Children enjoy learning traditional dances. They also enjoy dressing up and taking part in festivals.

# Past and present culture

**Culture** is the way we live. It is the clothes we wear, the foods we eat, the music we enjoy, the stories we tell, and the ways we celebrate. Italy is rich in culture. Everywhere you look, there are historic buildings and museums filled with art. There are ruins of buildings from long ago and statues of heroes from history. The most exciting part of Italy's culture, however, is how people celebrate it today. Italians love to celebrate their history and culture!

*(top) In the town of Vigevano, famous historic games take place every year to remember the past. On the second Sunday of October, a special parade is held in front of the town's castle.*

*(bottom) These musicians have come from Brazil to Perugia to play their drums at the Umbria Jazz Festival.*

## The *Palio*

The *Palio* is an exciting religious and historic event that takes place in Siena. It is a horserace that is held twice each summer. The celebration begins when ten riders chosen from different areas of the city bring their horses into the church to be blessed. Before the race, the horses and riders parade in the streets with the townspeople, who are dressed in costumes from the past. People put on a great show with traditional costumes, music, and a colorful parade.

*Before the horserace begins, there is a parade.*

*The jockeys ride without saddles, making dangerous turns in the* piazza.

# Carnevale in Venice

The word *carnevale* means "goodbye to meat." The festival of *Carnevale* is celebrated before **Lent**. Lent is a 40-day period of prayer and fasting, when Roman Catholics in the past did not eat meat. A week or more before Lent, people dress in costumes. Some of the most spectacular costumes and celebrations can be found in Venice. These include parades and fancy dances called **balls**, to which people wear fantastic costumes and masks, like the ones shown on these two pages. Which costume do you like best?

# Italy's great artists

*This statue, called David, was created by Michelangelo, who was both a sculptor and a painter.*

Art has always been an important part of Italian culture, even in the earliest days, but Italy is best known for its **Renaissance** art. "Renaissance" means "rebirth." Art was reborn, or became more exciting, during this time. Renaissance artists such as Leonardo da Vinci, Michelangelo, and Sandro Botticelli used rich colors to make their paintings more beautiful. Many artists painted religious pictures on the walls and ceilings of churches.

*These beautiful works of art are on a ceiling in the Vatican Museum in Vatican City.*

*This painting is part of Botticelli's "Birth of Venus." Venus was the goddess of love and beauty in the ancient Roman religion.*

*This painting of an angel is on a wall of the Vatican. It was painted by a Renaissance artist.*

*One of Leonardo da Vinci's most famous works of art is the "Mona Lisa." People love her smile.*

# Italy's famous buildings

The buildings in Italy are also works of art. Many of Italy's greatest structures were built long ago. Some were built by the ancient Romans, and some were constructed later. Old buildings are often used as theaters and museums. Most old buildings are visited by **tourists** from Italy and other countries. A tourist is a person who visits places for fun. Enjoy visiting the buildings on these pages!

*The Verona Arena is an **amphitheater** that was built almost 2,000 years ago. An amphitheater is a round building without a roof, like a stadium. Huge opera performances and concerts are held in the arena. The show below is an opera called Aida. As many as 15,000 people can sit in the arena to watch it.*

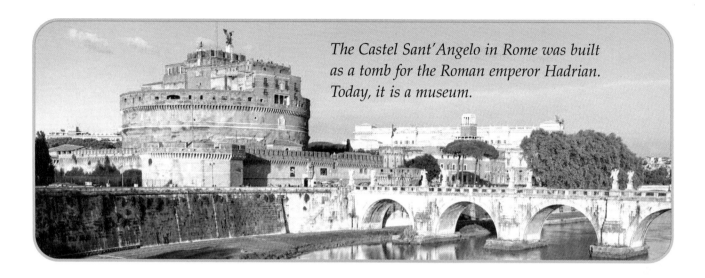

The Castel Sant'Angelo in Rome was built as a tomb for the Roman emperor Hadrian. Today, it is a museum.

Pisa's leaning tower was built in 1174. The land under it sank and caused the tower to lean.

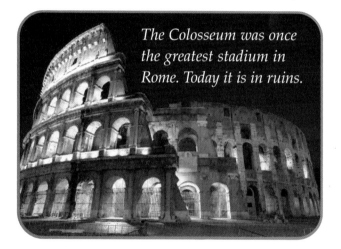

The Colosseum was once the greatest stadium in Rome. Today it is in ruins.

One of the largest **cathedrals** in Europe is Milan's Duomo. It can hold up to 40,000 people.

# Italian food

People all over the world love Italian food. Pizza, spaghetti, lasagna, and cannelloni are just a few popular Italian dishes. The foods on the right are some of the **ingredients** that are used to make these delicious foods.

pepper

garlic

basil

mozzarella cheese

pasta

spaghetti

provolone cheese

tomatoes

spices

*Spaghetti can be made with many vegetables, as well as with meatballs.*

*Pizzas can have different toppings. What toppings are on this pizza?*

Olive oil is used to make many foods. It is a very healthy oil. It tastes good on bread, too.

Lasagna is layers of meat, cheeses, and vegetable sauces between flat sheets of pasta.

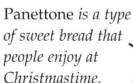

Cannelloni is made with pasta that can be filled with cheese or meat.

Panettone is a type of sweet bread that people enjoy at Christmastime.

Gelato is an Italian ice cream that comes in many colors and flavors.

31

# Glossary

**Note**: Some boldfaced words are defined where they appear in the book.

**active** Describing a volcano that has erupted recently or may soon erupt

**cathedral** A very large church

**conquer** To take over something forcefully

**continent** One of the seven large areas of land on Earth

**country** An area of land that has borders and a government

**empire** A large group of countries ruled by a single ruler

**extended family** Referring to family members that include more than just parents and their children

**first communion** A Roman Catholic ceremony in which children participate

**harbor** An area of water near a coast where boats are protected from wind and waves

**historic** Something that is important and teaches us how people lived in the past

**ingredients** Food items used to make different dishes

**lava** Magma, or liquid rock, which has erupted out of a volcano

**pasture** Land that is covered with grass on which animals feed

**peninsula** A piece of land that has water almost all the way around it

**pope** The head of the Roman Catholic Church

**valley** A flat area below mountains

**volcanic eruption** An explosion of lava, gases, ash, and rocks through a volcano

# Index